# THE WORLD GOES DOWN SLOW

# The World Goes Down Slow

*a poetry collection*

Ashley Logan

*For Brandon, my greatest adventure.*

# Contents

*Do I dare*
*Disturb the universe?*

*- T.S. Eliot*

**IN WHICH WE SIT IN THE GARDEN AND CONTEMPLATE GRIEF**

You pluck thin petals from a nearby yellow jessamine; fine, velvet things of gold; and gather them in your shaking, mindful hands. This is a tribute, performative, like rosary beads against your trembling fingers. Sitting in the flowerbed, you are surrounded, but it is not enough. Your name falls to your filthy knees that are kneeling as if in prayer among the ants and the beetles and the wayward spider that crosses over you, unbothered. Lick your lips, taste everything – there, an unearthing that starts with your fingers, now pressed into the dirt, searching. You say your name better than anyone but find it is stuck in the back of your throat, pieces sloughed from your tongue and swallowed like a pill without water. It burns while it dissolves, and you work your esophagus with anxious violence as a black butterfly finds its home on your body, transferred from flight to fury, wings twitching in the breeze. You yearn to touch those, too, sure they'd be soft, but you refrain as you do in all things and close your eyes against the temptation. It is one thing to feel vacant and another thing entirely to be so empty as to not know grief. And you do know grief as you sit vulnerable and alone with such tiny life that is somehow larger than you can comprehend. You open your eyes and trace the sycamore trees on the horizon, moved by their enormity. This is not the ending you expected, this sling of invocations made verbal as you hum and sigh. Casting the amber petals up, up into the air, they float, transfixed, and you with them, a signal that not all is foregone, nature always listening to how your body speaks. Tiny earthquakes are found beneath your quickening hands and you start to call yourself home. You say your name now, a gentle vibration that turns the earth over in relief, burying you with the flowers: a simple funeral, a humble release. We are all but soil in the end.

## THE WORLD GOES DOWN SLOW

The world goes down slow,
      a gentle submersion.
            *Come alive,*

it says to the wildlife hiding
      beneath the longleaf pine
            with branches that signal peace

against a solemn dark. The world pauses in
      a moment of question. The blindness
            you feel is no accident. Sensing my curiosity,

animals scatter as quickly as they
      came, leaving me to wonder after,
            like the human I am.

To leap into this moment
      is to abandon the last, humanity
            in transition within our sights.

I am taught about losing
      through evolution; what is left is
            the ellipsis of pausing: between.

And with a macchiato mouth,
      I kiss my lover as though
            he can revive me, feed me

his lifesaving breath, so I swallow –
      the world easing on its haunches
            unhurried. This is what

it is to not worry anymore.
      At 1:00am in mid-February, I have
            discovered my own savagery

and feel beneath the sheets.
      My body has morphed
            into one I can now touch,

a guide of nature's moods.
      Yes, the world goes down
            slow because it knows

the people it takes to earn
   catastrophe. I suppose I do, too.
     *Come alive*, I speak into existence

as the earth wakes. Here comes my body,
   lurching. It has known
     violence and I am rage,

but the world will surely
   survive me. And so
     I weep. So I sleep.

# THE WATER NEVER CARED

*after "Reading Hart Crane In Naples" by Ariel Francisco*

In theory, I say, I am like a bird – I
covet my hollow bones and know
I am delicate enough for air, the
words of others like water
sliding off my feathers, but I never
believed it enough, you see, so I asked
for forgiveness when it was you
who brought it all down – this
question of falling or leaping – the
final deliverance bringing me to water
again, and so I float, float, never
to be bothered, despite who cared.

## GARDENING

A weed is simply any plant unwanted, and that makes me
think of how we respond to people, too.
I am no longer fooled by late summer blooms so
you can consider me unconflicted about what you are.
When you think of flowers, do you think of autumn?
As I do. Silver asters on the side of the highway
up the mountain, a poignant reveal of red and orange,
spoken from purple tongues. I am overwhelmed
because I have not listened before.
I am told to be a better gardener, and I am on my knees
in awe. I have found my god in the dirt and discovered that
even the prettiest iris is still a weed in the middle of a potato farm.
A lesson in humility, the tilling of judgement.
Clinging, clinging – flowers have sprouted
from between each vertebrae, a garden blooming
up my spine and into my skull as I consider connection.
I am made whole, strong, with every bud.
Unwanted, I embrace what it means to grow.

# GUILT

She couldn't breathe while
dressed in a raven's corpse,
choking on feathers as
she reached down her own
throat to open passageways,
She ate a rock thinking
it was a pearl, a paperweight
made of guilt and remorse.
This is the way it ends,
she thought, a small gulp
disguised as a breath,
the tiniest of sounds
from her open mouth
mistaken for a life birthed
of paper beaks, tiny bones
wrapped in skin and rind.
Vehemently she cried with
little lungs: a creation
unfolding like origami
upon her fingertips while
eyes locked upon the petite
wings stretching toward her
hungry mouth. Destroyed,
she swallows.

**ESCAPE**

*My world revolves around your love*, he graffitied the walls,
splintering me with each stroke.

This isn't what I hoped it would be, left beseeching
and broken on the fallowed ground. He

always left a mark, troubling, as he abandoned
all else for the sake of an impetuous

thrust. His love is transactional and fleeting,
orbiting his need, an indication of how small

he really is. Without me, this room is empty. *Without
me*. A thought I hold dear as we close the door.

## I SPY

I spy how the weeping
willows kiss the wet ground,
heavy, and I think of how
this is a happy little accident,

a Bob Ross painting, working.
Chickadees chirp as
cirrus clouds whisk the sky,
before, tails of tiny specters

that are witnessed in movement,
mute but forgiving. I spy
a stray cat on the fence
and name him after he is gone,

tired, but observing. It rained
for a week here, though even
now as the sun reveals itself,
I remain indoors, shut away.

I spy life from my bedroom
window at 8:00am, ritually,
and the dog excavates in bed,
the sheets a sheltering layer.

I am a storm wanting
to approach the land but
forced to pummel
the waves instead,

so I put on my face and spy
the way my body shifts and moves,
crashing but relenting, with
a word on my tongue: *behold.*

Surveilling, I can feel my mind
chase and my mouth opens
for a breath: a tempest rising,
a miniature gale between the lips.

# TRESPASS DURING THE DAY

Bodies shift in beds and send a signal
that restlessness comes for those who sin,
inescapable,
while chapped mouths gape,
a silent question breathed
through their lips
and in flight above
their heads,
a wanted spirit.
This is the way the night ends,
with dawn shackled to
fleshy ankles that rise, rise
in a shuffle and reach
towards bagels and coffee and eggs
while bleary-eyed and stirring.
The books on the kitchen counter
are thrillers, and pages of
dread and terror rescind the calm
the morning is supposed to bring,
but those are just stories,
unlike the horror of waking
when we haven't slept at all.
Witness the calamity of this mess,
the way bony fingers curl
around their ribs and
dishevel what was already unkempt,
fractured frames beneath the skin
that repeat interrogations
about how much a body
can curl into itself before breaking,
before being transformed entirely into
what is both haunted and terrible.

## INDICATIVE OF THE LOST

I sit on the porch and listen to the chickadees,
so often named for their voice,
which always struck me as sweet,
eloquent destiny attached to their beaks.
I whisper, tempted by the notion.
The sun beats down on my thighs,
leaving a swift red birthmark across them,
a signature of kind. I am born in the daylight.
I straighten my arms overhead,
reach and stretch my body
like a piece of gum that clings to the tongue
and pushes its way from between these lips with a puff
to create the perfect bubble that pops at capacity,
of course it does, and then clutches the surface
of this mouth, that chin, this nose.
I pull the remnants from my face, a catastrophe of pink.
I press my sticky fingers into the burns of my legs,
watch as white dots bloom and fade
over and over again. I think to myself,
*surely, there is more here to remember.*

## GAPING, GIRL

We hiked in the dead of summer, dead on our feet, dead ahead.
We stroked between our breasts and swiped at the sweat pooled there,
this most sensitive spot. Climb, girl. We are not fooled, girl. A cavern
in your mouth, gaping, girl. Seek the forsaken and kiss their graves;
turn them, I'm sure, with sticky lips and porous teeth. We hear
our body speak, girl. Mourners stand by in hungry wake.
By September you'll have sewn your skin back into place
and smiled in response to the ones who have found safety,
kissed their fiends, and dissolved despite, despite. We reach the top
this time, forsaken the monsters to the abandoned, and breathe, girl,
while deciding what to do with this new knowledge,
a woman now,
who tastes herself.

## ENDINGS

I find myself looking out
the window often,
observing the way trees scratch
at the full blue sky,
a simple act of crooked coercion,
a small demand for reflection:
I serve as witness to this – &
also to the disintegration of ourselves
in this room, listening
to a kind of concentrated shattering
in the silence that sits with us.
So I watch little birds hop
along naked branches,
their little beaks widening
while deciding whether to take off or to stay,
and so I whisper: *go, go*.
I can see my likeness in the glass panes
but I can still see through me, too.
I am but invisible here,
looking out always while
feeling my own slight bones
freeze at the sight of such quiet liberty.
You watch me watch them, though.
I realize, hand pressed to glass,
that whatever end
we thought we were approaching
will never be
quite as we imagined.

# THINGS I'VE DONE TO AVOID THINKING

Climbed 500 feet of rock with nothing but the addiction
  to fear chasing my exposed back.
Hiked miles and miles of terrain to retrain my mind on how to forget.
Read a book about a dysfunctional family who would rather kill
  than talk to each other about how they felt.
Listened to the new Taylor Swift album, nodding my head to lyrics
  that felt familiar before I knew them.
Doomscrolled too much social media as the rot threatened
  my creativity.
Attacked my hair with scissors and dye in case a transformation in style
  would also reinvent my brain and the tide of my moods.
Created a bonfire in the lawn as the sun tired for the evening, flames
  licking at the arriving stars as if coughing over terrestrial secrets.
Avoided all my texts and calls that dripped with triggers and lies.
Debated on what could be considered the common denominator
  beneath all the exhaustion: is it me or is it me.
Cried a lot, discovered that I do still feel despite my best efforts
  and scheming.
Wrote poetry in the stunted word by word dance of not knowing
  what to say.
Lost my safety in the noise and neglected to recall that the only person
  who will protect my peace is me.
Gifted myself with knowing my endings are also my beginnings.
Remembered to hold space for thoughts, for healing, for life.
Held space for myself −
  and made no apologies for becoming the person I've always needed.

## AND SO WE GRIEVE

I grieve for us
in the same way clouds
lament their weight,
crying now,
soaking everything.
I question whether
I have leapt or I have fallen,
this broken horror
a wretched symptom
of defeated love,
something we found
beneath all the years
and all the trying.
Bent and disturbed,
our wounded mouths
are muted in response
to the wreckage,
the storm swell predicted
yet weathered inside
these shattered,
shuttered bodies.
We remain witness
in the wake: the way
the sun desiccates,
after, so like us,
an emptying of hearts.

## SMALL TOWN REFLECTIONS

I sneak up on myself, a reflection caught
in the windowed sun, with a look
of surprise captured in glass
as I witness myself emerge.
How like life. This palace
may be broken, but I
am made of the jointed.
I am not so startled as
I duck into the dark,
the door left open behind me,
an invitation. The unfamiliar attacks me
but I resist: a catastrophe of senses.

I gave up my body in a small town
in order to feel used, something I
think about now as I enter
the exploited. I didn't need drugs
with thrills of choice in my veins.
How like now. I've discovered my worth
by standing alone, comforted by
the echoes of those who have gone:
a privilege to be made into change.

We are only as grounded
as what we leave behind.
And so I sit in the rubbish,
finding my name for the first time.
Say it aloud. Witness the dust
that stirs. How like me.

# CONSEQUENCE

Beneath my right shoulder
blade is a wound. It pains me
from time to time, cause unknown,
a fierce reminder that my body
still has secrets. It does not bleed,
this wound. Sometimes what hurts
is not wrong after all. We adapt.
I think about my mother who
does not sleep, who shuffles in the dark.
She would say it is without purpose.
With wilted wrists, my hands hover,
and search. Sometimes what is wrong
does not hurt. My family is made
of the untold, and I am no different.
There is a language for it, home.

## I DREAMT OF A WOMAN

I began to bleed
when I was eleven and
became afraid that
someone might see,
so I never spoke of it:
ashamed of myself
for becoming a woman
when the world seemed
to despise us so.
I discovered myself
in the echo of mirrors
when I was thirteen,
dissociated but whole
and no longer forbidden,
from feeling my worth,
from touching my body.
I traced my jawline
in the glass and smiled
with chiseled teeth:
pronounced, finally,
and gaping with promise.
I became a connoisseur
of deep sunsets early
because I saw myself
in the way the day bled.
Give them all to me.
I'll swallow them whole
as the earth does the day,
my scarlet throat working:
shades of confidence
betraying the youth that
taught me to be afraid
of what I could be.
I am now thirty-five,
fingers tracking the valleys
of my hips, sorting through
the weeds of my bush,
rising over the hills of
my breasts: blushing
from use rather than
shame. My name is
now a prayer caught
on the lips of lovers,

tongues finding my center,
tasting: still, I bleed.

# THERE IS NO SUCH THING AS NOTHING

not in this body.

The center of my abdomen and the curve of my ankles
and the notches of bone in my neck and every little knuckle.

The focus of the universe is found
behind the treeline veins of my eyes
but also in the bullfrog outside my window

and also in the pink of your palms and
also in the hungry summer heat.
You smile and say you love it here.

My temperament understands more now
that the past is no longer accosted by it.

There is no such thing as nothing: not in this world.

I spell beauty on your lips and can taste myself,
and this is how I know. The rearrangement of these words
rearranges the universe, and I am but one – centered.

# RELIGION FOUND IN A CORPSE-CANDLE
*after Outlander: Dragonfly In Amber*

She stumbled upon a corpse with bright, blue fungus
thriving over his thin, white skin. They preserved
his body like flowers in a vase: beautiful yet departed.
She recalled how a soldier said once, "It makes you wonder
where they live between battles." The thought
brought me to my knees, fingers searching
the soil furtively for seeds that do not exist:
a glimpse at how little we know beyond ourselves.
I can picture how the blossoms would look permuting
from my hands, vivid blooms cascading across
my bony wrists and reaching towards my stilled bosom.
This is how fiction is created, an image plucked
and pressed like petals, captured and reinvented.
I am not her. But she is all of us, facing
the certainty that is death though buoyed by tiny miracles.
It is, after all, how we approach faith. Often too tired to listen,
we find dogma in the blooms that emerge from our bodies.
Perhaps that is why our veins run blue under our skin,
a whisper yet – of what is to come, of what has transpired.

## GHOSTS IN THE LIGHT

When you think of ghosts,
do you think of me? I am
the tick you hear of the clock,
a small sound that belies
presence of body. Mine is
torturous, a process to forget.
I sit and become less. As the sun
beams glare through
window blinds at dawn,
I can see dust hover,
fairies in the light – slowly
pirouetting, a deathly spectacle.
This reminds me that spirits
are more than what assails us:
they are also of us, an accord
of hauntings. What we have
become is a passage of unkind,
adrift souls. I am undone,
and your life sheds itself
upon my weary sights,
twirling, a display of ifs.

# TO THE RUINS OF ME

I am told you cannot run from yourself,
a truth that became stuck between
my teeth, wedged and chewed the
more I spoke, ate, breathed.

I escaped to the Alps of Germany
in order to feel small, but instead
I was transformed by the rock, a
quiet story of becoming. I spelled
my name in the cracks, discovered
eternity with my hands, my tongue.
How large I feel. How small I am.

Romania's countryside sang
a hymn that I could believe,
and I balanced my mind in
the still waters of Venice.

The stray cats in Rome came free
to my hands. They rubbed their
little bodies against my palms,
and I thought about worth,
how much of it I could stand.

I pick at my teeth now with my tongue.
I feel how hard the truth has become.

## THE BIRDS OF RECKONING

Sycamore trees, like ethereal sentinels,
wait for their color to turn over while standing stark
against the water's edge. A reach of branches dressed in silk
above me; my feet buried in the cold mud.
I once fed myself to anyone who saw me.
So which say more – our palms or our faces?
I suspect I can be read, a contraction of lines
spelling my name: two syllables, spoken best by me. I press
my hand to my cheek, a solemn affair
because my touch is still the only one I crave.
I find the egret on the rocks ahead,
a blue silhouette that shifts with me, lifting wings
that have been carved from my bones.
The sycamore trees have not moved though they move me.
I continue to feed myself to the birds and am swallowed
by hundreds of feathered throats,
a surrender in the canal where two rivers meet.
I remember my taste and feel honor in sharing.
I can be retained, significance resting upon my tongue
and home is found in the question of my skin, shed here.
The guardians surround me as a wisp of breeze
lifts what is left of my body. What is left
is my heart, plunged deep in the waters to be reborn.
The trees whisper in ghost languages but I
am not alarmed that I understand. I say I am a bird,
but my body is defiant even as it transforms.
A question of whether I will be remembered.

## DEER CYCLONE

I was a romantic child –
an unfurled deer surrounded
by a sanctuaried herd.
I discovered the magic of family
between and within words,
a collection of language yet pronounced
though eternally learned.
Words were my first love because
they taught me that love existed at all. I yearned
for requitedness: passion and ardor
and frenzied lust. The kind that
would leave me both breathless and breathing.
The kind found between trees, the quiet
movement of familiarity and freedom
that taught of both escape and surrender.
As an adult, I cocooned myself in my belief
like reindeer protecting its fawn –
circling and circling –
creating a cyclone of refuge
in a beautiful maneuver of one:
of both the shielded and the shielder.
I found romance there. In our breath,
the warm mist in the cold, absconded from
our bodies – evidence revealed, a rooted tale of love
in the brush collected upon our hungry tongues.

## MY FIRST KISS

occurred in the branches of a tree,
my face upturned as though my mouth
would capture the sky on my lips – finding
a boy instead. As I stood on the cliffs
of Shortoff Mountain, I remembered
how that kiss felt like being on the edge:
wind pushing my back toward a fall. But I
remained steady, feet planted like stubborn
cedar trees emerging from the fringe of rock, and
I spoke of memory, how it alters us as much as
the experience of things. My last kiss was at a campsite
by the fire, a spark by a spark. As my tongue felt
for grounding in his mouth, I recalled how we
met a hawk at the summit of our hike.
Watched his effortless flight caught in the wind
and thought about the difference between taking
versus giving. How the effort feels the same but
the outcome is never the stuff we hope for.
My next kiss will be with a man I'm devoted to,
and it's like the hard climb you take to the top
of a mountain: your muscles work and ache,
your lungs breathless with exertion, but you still
manage a small gasp at the view, one breath, stolen
when there is no air. The difference between
learning and loving. How it gathers what is left.

## WHAT I MISS

Start the day:
        shoveling fog into your mouth for breakfast.

The mist of the morning curls in your stomach
        and drifts between your lips, a swallow away

from hardening, a pellet upon the altar.
        Recall: it begins in the pit below your ribs,

that sensitive spot where the blades slice
        cleanly, quick, neat: a cavity gaping for circumstance.

I remember now. How the ache pings after,
        an echo that can almost be heard as it settles

like haze in the sunlight. Even the fog has its dawn.
        I hear it: the beginning. The haunt of day recedes,

and I yearn for the kind of pain that has no origin.
        You discover it: here. Turn it over. Eat that, too.

# A SONG IN THE KAYAK OF MOURNING

You point out the northern parula's trill
    to me as we cut through the water,
birthed in the sunlight: the rising song
    with the final sharp note. The yellow warbler
not yet tentative of us. This is the harmony
    I will remember when I am gone –
certain, I am, as I watch colors flick through,
    a discovery of movement. Speak to me of birds,
and I will commit their voices to memory
    because you loved them. We brush hands
as we pass, pathways carved in our fluid wake –
    fringed, temporary. Our reflections stir
beneath, broken. Do not grieve. My body is caught
    alive, but there are hawk feathers in the water.
Your children will sprout wings from their spines,
    a tribute to invincible youth. What we find here
will become home in the oaks. You point to me and
    the trill is quiet. The final note, a question.

## NATURE WALKS

Picture it:
a camouflaged moth
resting on a concrete wall.

I ask if she feels safe.

Her brown and tan wings
a stark reply to the white
surroundings.

When is the last time

someone asked her that?
The moth twitches.
She is not where she should be,

(or) she is not blending in,
which says more about
us as neighbors than it does
about her ability to hide

in the plainest of sights.

# SHAPESHIFTER

*"I want to throw a party for the heartbreak
that turned you into a poet." - Mindy Nettifee*

I am a shapeshifter, shadows of previous lives
gathered in a singular place and haunched
under street lamps as the dark drags the day
back into the light. Thrust forward, it comes slowly,
the sky iridescent in its struggle, and yet:
I am in awe, urging. I am saddened by my lacking
as though my body was formed with an unhoned blade,
imperfect. The silhouettes retreat and I stand naked
in the brilliance of noon. I've habitually written words
through heartbreak, a practiced effort of placing language
before thought and thought before feeling, but
I became a poet when my lives broke apart – scattered
like confetti in a breeze, leaving behind this one life:
broken, but here, nevertheless. I am a note of history,
the source of which has become a bouquet of lives,
though I grieve for what I have yet to lose.
Shadows trail as I walk back into the night,
arriving as it has with the same struggle as the day,
overturning itself like finger-paintings hung to dry.
My words are the same, dripping from my lips: a rouge
of becoming – risen in sensitivity, settled by savagery.

## TESSELLATION

The honeycombed earth tessellates
on the horizon, modeling wholeness
with a naked prayer of becoming.
Loneliness is when we have forgotten ourselves,
and so I search with my hands in the dirt.
I've yet to find my body, but I have found
skeletons beneath my nails, between my teeth.
The grit lingers and so I swallow the spirit
with the spit. Hungry for identity.
The pattern for discovery is an invention made
by the ignorant though there is no shame
in the learning, in the trying. Perhaps
the earth will devour me as I have consumed it.
Galvanized, I leap, which is to say
I am not falling but flying. A fair trade:
listen to how her body speaks, quaking
as I disturb her once more.
We meet where the sky climaxes,
a determined question
perfected in want.

# BEHIND THE CURTAIN

A healing inner child sits
behind this heart's curtain,
anxiously picking at her knuckles
as she peers out from behind the folds,
casting a frightened glimpse at
what all I've done since her span.
There is no explanation for
adding up the days: only time.
It is cruel, how this heart hides
from itself – battered and unwilling.
Behind the curtain, the child
does not cry. Instead, she whistles
a tune for me – waiting, waiting.
When the curtain finally lifts,
the scenery has fallen apart,
a catastrophe of experience.
I greet her. Lift her. Beseech her.
My heart pounds with the effort
while suddenly exposed in crisis.
So much time has passed that
she fails to forgive me, fails to
recall that she is me, only: revealed.
Trauma has a way of licking away
the memory but never the wounds.

## PRESCRIBED BURN

I can hear the collapse of what was
crackle in the quiet forest, the way
the earth yearns for the chance to
be renewed in place, a chance for
the pinewood ecosystem to thrive.
I can't help but also think about how
I couldn't love myself for loving him.
Choked by all that was invasive,
I had just this one chance to finally,
potentially – live. The ashes from him
are soft under my feet. Soft in a way
I never knew him to be. I look
behind me and the flames lick,
then devour, all within my path
as the drip torch balances
on my hip and feeds the ache
of transformation. Growth is a
lifestyle of survival, as evidenced
by all that is blackened here.
The smoke offers ghosts, moving slowly,
quietly, in a breeze that fills the lungs.
I breathe it in so that I can remember
how much this burns me, too.
Rebirth is not passive. The ghosts here
are not just of them but of us, of me.
Eerie in their silence, complete
in a way we never were. I watch as we
become past tense, now as I did then.
My lungs are ablaze with wretched weight
as I struggle for the limited clean air.
But there is also relief because
there is only this ending, an overture
into retrieving my body and my mind.
Violence has found its way home, but
I am ignited, too. I leave the ash where it lies.
Where it belongs – beneath and behind.

# CHILDHOOD

Barefoot, run across the asphalt as quickly
as you can, child, for it is hot, so hot.
Bounce from one foot to the other, hopping,
the floor is lava, child. Run through the grass,
feel its cool fingers tickle your toes, yes,
that's the stuff, of dirt and clay. Run –
across the sand, run towards the water, run
as though you're being chased. Run, child, run.
The bottoms of your feet were made to be tough
because vulnerable is a word you have
not yet learned. Your feet were built for this,
child, darkened by the earth so that you could
become strong and willful in her image.
Carry forward. Your feet will become soft
with age as you forget all of this. You will
discover what it is to be vulnerable,
what it means to feel exposed, so you will
walk instead of run one day. But not this day,
child. Barefoot, run across the pavement, feel
the burn of the day linger on your skin again.
This will haunt you, child, this will fortify you:
remember how it feels to understand the
land because you've bared yourself for it,
a promise to return your body to its god.

## THE DIFFERENCE

is it your life that is aflame or does everyone
need to be scorched in order for you to feel
honest? about your mistakes, we should examine
that which refuses to burn. piles of all
you would love to be rid of, every person who
you have wronged remain standing in the ashes,
resistant to your ire. even when ignored, the past
continues to become. though your pattern is
a refusal of accountability, we can see you still:
a figure created by mirrors, an absorption of image,
but fragile and duplicitous all the same.
nothing can thrive in the invasive rot of your fraud.
i have not forgotten because the fumes reek,
creating a layer of smog adrift, signaling the ruination
you invented yet refuse to own despite your hands
dripping with torched gasoline. a pity that you
cannot burn, too, for maybe then you would have
a chance at not only survival but maybe also growth.
someone more humane would be able to see
that the difference between chimney smoke and
a forest fire is the destruction left behind.

## THE DIFFERENCE
*a blackout poem experiment*

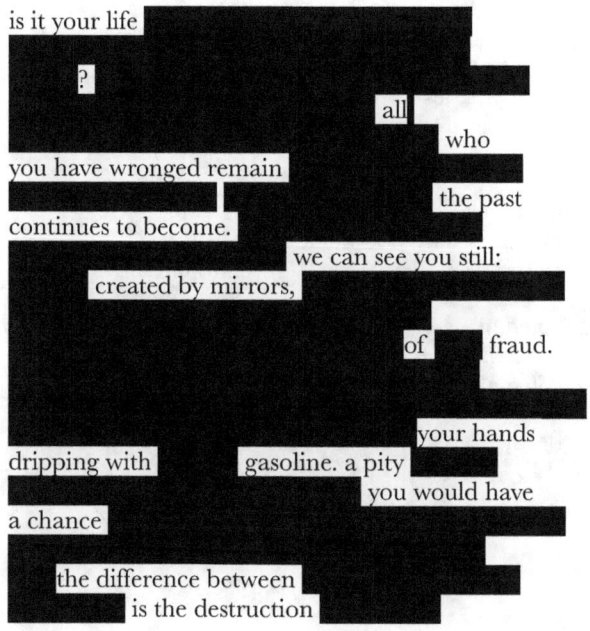

is it your life
?
all
who
you have wronged remain
the past
continues to become.
we can see you still:
created by mirrors,
of        fraud.
your hands
dripping with        gasoline. a pity
you would have
a chance
the difference between
is the destruction

\*\*\*

[is it your life?
all who you have wronged remain;
the past continues to become.
we can see you still:
created by mirrors, of fraud.
your hands dripping with gasoline.
a pity, you would have a chance.
the difference between
is the destruction]

47

## PEEK

I found a picture of an eyeball online
with veins that stretched and curved,
winter oaks in a forest.          How amazing

to glimpse the wild that pervades
behind our eyelids, a complicated but humble
jungle birthing what is ocular, singular.

The untamed parts of myself
are reflected in mirrors that I dare not touch
for I was taught my skin is forbidden,          even to me.

So, I seek out abandoned places          dilapidated churches,
decrepit train depots, derelict homes
and they remind me of my body.

We are also built to decay.

# I NO LONGER DREAM AT NIGHT

Bodies shift in beds and send a signal
that restlessness comes for those who sin,
inescapable,
while chapped mouths gape,
a silent question breathed
through their lips
and in flight above
their heads,
a wanted spirit.
This is the way the night ends,
with dawn shackled to
fleshy ankles that rise, rise
in a shuffle and reach
towards bagels and coffee and eggs
while bleary-eyed and stirring.
The books on the kitchen counter
are thrillers, and pages of
dread and terror rescind the calm
the morning is supposed to bring,
but those are just stories,
unlike the horror of waking
when we haven't slept at all.
Witness the calamity of this mess,
the way bony fingers curl
around their ribs and
dishevel what was already unkempt,
fractured frames beneath the skin
that repeat interrogations
about how much a body
can curl into itself before breaking,
before being transformed entirely into
what is both haunted and terrible.

# SPIDER-WEBS AND DISHWATER

Found in the dingy dishwater,
the gathering puddles on the porch,
the decay of the day continues on.
I've counted the hours with
fatigued fingers. An aberrant call
for something else is thrown out
the cracked windows and tumbles
to the feet of passers-by who
step over, step around, step until
left behind. Cross-stitched eyes
of blue watch unblinking and hands
proffer every thing ever once held,
a shadowed gesture. Underneath
fingernails, my own skin, brought
to my lips and cleaned with my teeth:
consumed. The draw is pulling me back,
and I have given in. The day turns
itself over eventually. Meanwhile.
Isn't this what it is to live? I ask.
Skipping out into the night, entangled
in the silvery threads of web, yes.

# THINGS I'M TRYING TO COME TO TERMS WITH

My brain is both my brain and not my brain, at once
wild and feral, at once subdued and desperate. The names
I have answered to: crazy, emotional, unpredictable and
predictable alike, *too* insert-verb-here. Acceptance of
every perspective and perception but my own. All
the guilty pleasures I no longer feel guilty about,
like the books, the desserts, the loves I fostered
and then let go — searching, longing. The inability to
know what I was looking for, only that I've been looking.
Wandering. The losing of my self, over and over and over —
a plummet I can never avoid into a chilled pool of waterfall,
observing as everything I built tumbles over the edge
after, crashing into brokenness upon my half-submerged
Head. Eyes turned up to watch the fall but unable to stop
it. Witnessing. My overgrown garden a burial ground of
every fresh start and the abandoned senses that used to be
mine — before. My brain is both my brain and not my brain.
Endlessly, I create these ghosts; I determine what lives.

## UNCONTAINED

In the name of love, my feelings
were beaten from erasers
behind our home, the chalk
of me a furious swarm, swept
away by the shuffle of feet. I
witnessed myself in the prints
across the floor, a trail leading
to every moment I was silenced.
In the name of love, I became
convinced there was nowhere for
my hope to land. A wisp of a woman,
the defect of caring started to dull
and drift, my mind unable to remain
engaged. But now, as time gathers,
a revival – my hands covered
in dust from swiping clean all
those previous graves. I run
my fingers across my mouth, curious.
In the name of love, discovery.
In the name of love, myself.
Quick, a dart of earnest tongue
followed by a birthing, filthy smile.

## MEMORIES I'D LIKE TO BOTTLE

Snow over the Grand Canyon. His skin
beneath my lips. The tiny wings of a butterfly
fluttering beside my ear, head in the grass,
fingers tangled in my bush. Moments of
clarity, of hope, of joy – often brought on
after sweaty hikes in the summer, the breeze
gently moving the hair that clings to our necks.
I need to bottle every scent and sound,
like the snort of laughter that surprises us both,
the way his thick fingers feel trailing my hipbones.
It is unfair to have to rely on something as fragile
as memory to contain us. To contain this, echoes
of my days. Birds calling from tall trees, nephews
crying out in excitement, so pleased. Meeting
new friends at baseball games, the chants and chatter
during autumn tailgates. The crowded streets of
London and Rome and New York, the countrysides
of Romania and Germany. Finding peace in the
mountains, remembering the unknowable in oceans,
and being comforted beneath vast skies. If only I could
bottle it all so when memories fail, as they do and warp
and fade, I could relive it all. A comfort to retrieve
the souvenirs of experience that remind me of myself.
Of the life I have lived. And that I – in fact – have lived.
Though, mostly, what I wish for is to be able to look back
and say: I still feel the same.

## DEVASTATED IN SWATHS OF COLOR

Yarrows bloom from between my teeth,
and I swallow seeds meant to be planted.
I drink water and water and water until I am filled,
my skin soaked, though my eyes dry.
I can see others pretend I have not arrived,
my words buried beneath their muddy feet
as they run towards the life I am not meant to know.
But the sun casts shadows as much as it sheds light,
and I am understood, heard, seen within this land of birth.
I carve myself into bartered bark,
both devastated and deserved.
I see myself in the color green,
a signal of how I'm nascent and hopeful.
Soil is found beneath my nails in all the ways
I have touched experience. I am gathered in your hands,
a bouquet of trying. Pink and yellow and purple
rest on my tongue, and I smell the scent of familiarity.
Reciprocity spills itself upon your fingertips,
which I meet with my own. They touch my hair,
locks of revolution, and I smile — for I am spring.

# HOW TO KEEP GOING

Do you see the way the buds
break in the spring? No matter
what the winter did to us,
they startle in green, a shock
of color that says: *stay*. Imagine,
yourself, a bud. Capable of
transformation from frost to
thaw, coming alive, rising.
The skeletons of trees renew
every year, just as your body
awakens each pass around
the sun, a day that says: *you
made it*. Breaking apart,
do you see your red message?
A bud blooming into life, again,
despite. In spite. Miraculous,
every time. Take a breath:
you are the pause before
the *amen*. Stunning, you break
open, the warm light of spring
a taste on your budding tongue.

*after Sylvia Plath*
## SUMMER ENDS LIKE

weeping, slowly and painfully with an ache
that stubbornly clutches to your sternum.
the green of august begins to curl on
the tongue, a fervent taste of conclusion
that, if held there, lingers like morning dew.
before the startling heat of a sun rising,
as though our timing is premature in its desire.
the odd uneven time, somehow both over
and begun as an ellipsis of birds sit atop
the line overhead, pausing. shaky breaths
escape into cooled lungs as the land settles in
both sigh and shudder. summer ends like love:
once fierce and then slowly, suddenly, gone.

# DREAMSCAPE

My grandmother asks how I like to take my coffee,
and I tell her just a little bit of honey is fine, please,
as we settle at the kitchen table, and she then asks
how my writing is going, and I tell her how I create
memories with her ghost, pouring from an invisible
pot to fill our cups, and this is grief, I think,
speaking through me as though my god is sorrow
and sorrow is my god, and she understands
this without me having to explain, so she
pushes a pen towards me and tells me to go,
but I linger and watch for the knowing smirk,
a comma etched into her face, forever
forming a pause in which we can meet, and
so I take my leave, and she bids me farewell,
and memory manages to find us in the abstract,
this place, doesn't it, or so I've found, but
my grandmother would know as she clears the table
and pours the coffee down the sink with a wink.

## SPECIAL PROBLEMS IN VOCABULARY

*after Tony Hoagland*

Where does language go as a heart quietly breaks?
What is the word for digging through the cavities
of your mind and finding that all healing must be
done alone? How do I describe the tragic realization
that my body is not safe? That my worth is observed
and decided in front of men and mirrors? What is the
verb for when dawn sunlight kisses and soothes
the aching face of a woman who sobbed for mercy?
I wonder about the word for when laughter finally
escapes from a raw throat, that gnarly feeling scraping
up and out for release. Poetry is the steady excavation
of hindsight. Have I ever come close to understanding?
Unearthed, the discovery that adjectives are in everything
I am and was and will be. How my hands hold yours
in grief and in love, a tether. Breaking apart and holding
space for the pieces, a kindness. Vocabulary finds me
as my legs tire from walking, destination everywhere,
anywhere, while fiery lungs despair for breath. But look:
how small we can become. How small we've always been,
like fireflies dotting the summer woods, our little words
brightening and dimming in a tapestry of cadence.
Beckoning us home, language gently returned.

## HOT GIRL SHIT

buying books to add to the stack piling next
to the bookshelf. changing the lightbulb that
went out months ago. walking without purpose.
singing badly to 90s playlists while driving.
wearing old panties on laundry days. reading
all about the curly girl method. vegging on
hummus and wine. traveling to chase the gifts
of getting lost. finding your own hair everywhere.
learning about boundaries. unearthing your voice
and practicing its sound. cuddling with your dog.
laughing until it burns your lungs, the most joyful
of hurts. remembering how to ride a bike.
letting go of expectations. in this body.
dancing in the yard with your sister then. and now.
renting your first place alone. investing in skin care.
crying over videos of lonely animals. admiring sunsets
out on the water, deep in the woods. becoming
present. divorcing and deciding what you deserve
out of love. out of life. writing it down: more.

## TAKING IT BACK

I could make a list of all the things I'm taking back, but the list is long and filled with all the things you'd expect (like my boundaries, my personhood, my ever-loving womanhood). It would include my hauntings, my dreams, everything I once said I wanted, my healing inner child, my words, my agency and finances, my sexuality, my body, my holy grail of intimacy. I'd include my name evolving into more, my needs and unraveled pleasure, my adventure, my creativity, my health, this path. Recall my safety and protection, the ability to change and evolve, my perspective, my validity, my self, my endings, my beginnings. Taking back 34 years and discovering who I relinquished and who I salvaged are not the same. Taking back every spurious day, curling them into my hands and feeling the way my will to live was always fragile, jagged edges barely memorized for all they were. Taking back all the hands that ever grazed my skin and thought they had left a meaningful mark, my history. Every second I shrank inside to become comfortable with being small in order to make someone else feel worthy. Taking back fragments and gifting myself the honor of being vulnerable inside truth, no matter how painful it may be to stand both splintered and perceived. Taking it all back and producing the kind of revenge that comes with finally living (if I were to make such a list).

## AN ODE TO PASSION

Reincarnate me into a bottomless body of water
where I can take all of you, over and over, and
be the absolver of the sins that fell from our lips.
We'd sink into the cenote below, a beautiful cavity
with shafts of light from above feeding our open
mouths, an invitation like fingers grazing the gap
of a secret doorway. Hidden only because worthiness
is gifted and then swallowed. Found only when
suspended in relief, this aching transformation that
hungrily devours and feeds on the tempting depths.

## &

In the gold of the ampersand,
a note finds its way
from your hand to mine
— symphony.
An upheaval of red
as your tongue
slides in my mouth.
Pardon me.
The sparrows have more to say
now than ever
as their little beaks emerge
— open, frail — and yet.
Unable to change a thing.
Our eyes find their bodies.
What benefits us?
In the amber, cicadas
mate and then die,
a moment everyone
must think about
— at least once.
I'm sorry.
We just want to be
found, a conjunction
that pieces this together.
And becomes then.

## ABOUT TREES

Speak to me about cathedral trees, how they grow
like a family from the same root cambium,
how you can step inside their circle and
feel small among the clustered redwoods but also
feel safe within their protection.
They remind me of you. I have no family
but I have been fortified here,
in the lines of my fingertips that press to your lips.
You can taste me.
We stand within our collar,
the perfect horizon untouched. I suppose
this is a love poem after all, an epigraph
dedicated and inscribed. Tell me
the difference between the shortleaf and
the longleaf pine, the length of their needles,
the size of their cones, the shape of their bark,
how much they grow. Remind me of
your favorite flower as our bodies meet,
bulbs expanding in a shock of color, a sensation
best felt than said. Speak to me often
about trees and I will find us there.
Nurtured, I will find us in everything.

# DON'T PICK THE FLOWERS

He told her once
that he preferred the wildflowers,
the evening primrose and the silver aster,
to the more famous blooms.

Wild though they were,
their names conjured between his lips,
names he whispered in her ear:
a secret only they were strong enough to know.

She allowed the wild to blossom in the back of her jaw,
chiseled teeth clenched and feral.
They tread across the meadow.

He dared not pick a flower for her;
she hated their little deaths.
Instead — he held out his hand,
and she could feel nature's grasp.

## A DAY IN THE WOODS

Witness how we plant young trees
with dibble bars, pressing and pulling,
creating a home like a deity in the dirt.
When you removed your hat
to wipe your face, a glistening veneer
beneath the sun, it was easy then to say,
*I love you*. I was moved by your power,
bending and pushing, and I, the tiny being,
recalled how hard you work inside me, too.
Moved, I say, against you and with you.
Witness how we plant ourselves firmly,
a prayer. When you straighten to observe
your work, we can see the future of the trees,
a hundred years of youth before us.
How like god. We find ourselves observed
as the woods surrender their message
of connection between effort and
sustenance. When you turn to me,
it is easy to say, *use me*, because I
am built to be your sanctuary.
Witness how you kneel, saying my name
as only you can, and your filthy hands
find me in the bright light, counting
every freckle like a rosary bead leading
to the cross between my breasts.
Listening to how my body speaks.
We are but two godlets in the woods,
a refuge. I understand now why we
keep planting – controlling what is
difficult, yearning for what is ours.
A world, no small creation.

## LITTLE DEATHS

Kissing graves between your legs
with gaping caverns, porous teeth clench
around the rise of ecstasy in a frenzy, and I
accept your little death in the back of my throat,
spelling your name with my tongue, for
we are only meant to dive off cliffs for the mourners.

## SACRIFICE

I tried to recreate the night
but tore the page with the weight
of stars I punched through it.
Which brings to mind the heaviness of
holding up the sky for you. An illusion.
This version of you that existed in short bursts,
a bright fairytale that I swallowed whole,
jaws unhinged to capture all you would have
me believe. Just long enough to keep me
addicted, returning, forgiving — a tide
answering to its moon. But also like the tide,
I have endured. So, I would rather drown
in the past to own my withheld fury and
declare the sacrifice to be my best decision,
even as the waves of repercussion rise.
Yet, you — in the end, you would dare
to shame the ocean for its wrath.

## LAVENDER

I came to recently with several hours gone, my body a vessel
spinning slowly atop the current, unfeeling but for the disoriented
blink that slammed me back into place.
I glanced at my hands and thought about how octopuses turn lavender
when they die, the chromatophores in their skin pulsing for hours after.
A wonder.
My skin does no such thing, signals none of the throbbing
behind my eyes as my legs tingle in the rumble of an approaching train.
The wind caresses my face, whips my hair – lilac stars
bursting in my vision. I can feel colorful tendrils
stretch out from my center, grasping.
Every waking has me monitoring for that lavender palette
as though I will know before it's too late,
something like hope.
My small world is transformed
by a more dominant force that turns me over:
either to love or to bury. A decision not yet made.
I glide forward in a vibrant plum fog to join the throngs
of both the confident and the stumbling.
My shuttered inhale is pushed back out in a whisper,
observing: "Look at everyone trying."

## IF I AM 60% WATER, THEN 40% IS...

laughter / wine and bread and tacos / thoughts
running wild like 'would my boyfriend still love me
if I were a worm?' / bleach and hair dye / roadtrips,
music, windows down / painful madness / grace
and forgiveness / fog lifting beneath the sun's gaze
/ the wind controlling the storm / raging waves that
destroy and the unmoving steadiness of mountains /
organized bookshelves and adventure itineraries /
ink from collected pens and tattoos / empty journals
/ yet so many words they can't help but leak from
my eyes / grief, a supple tree / a dark room of strangers
and ghosts / but also friends / also love / also also also

## I'M OKAY WITH

I am okay with becoming feral, a nymph of the trees,
the forest a place for shedding one life for another,
existing as the dew that washes little bird feet clean
before taking flight from steadfast branches, the feathers
that create thunderclaps in their flutter and lift,
the earth that shudders and shakes with all it has had
to endure, groaning and growing, the remaining nature
undeterred in the end, growing into both the warning
and the prayer, the woman and the goddess, the scream
that rises far above these woods as the roots shift
and stretch beneath, altered and uncontained,
finally refusing to become less.

# QUIET

The quiet specific to falling dark is my favorite kind of quiet. You can stand beneath a canopy of slowly shadowing trees, outlines defined by a bright moon, its craters like thumbprints pressed into the landscape of a painting. You can watch as small bats zip and swoop in the sheltered night, swiftly capturing insects in their mouths like stealthy acrobats twisting in a beautiful dance of hunger. I can feel my hunger rise in response, a slow grumble that echoes in my mouth as it falls open, prepared to eat the night. The nocturnal birds begin their haunt, chuck-will's-widows and whip-poor-wills competing throughout the pines while frogs take up their chorus in nearby pools. The quiet specific to earth and its creatures is the quiet we will hear as nature brings us home, burying us in the soil, where perhaps we will appreciate how precious silence is and everything we have yet to learn.

## SUMMIT

Though I am tethered
to the rock, I can feel
my body sway in the wind,
its guidance unrelenting.
I look down on a sailing hawk,
the sunlight revealing
the texture of its wings –
we are so fragile, at the mercy
of nature but mercy must be
vast and kind today, giving away
the magic outside our human jails.
Exposed, I have improvised
careful choreography atop
this mountain cascade
with hands feeling, feet carrying,
mind cracking open to strip
and release all else away.
Experience is the drug coveted,
mental groundwork begun
as my feet depart the earth
beneath. I dance, then pause,
breath whisked away by
insistent mortality – yet my body
is full. I can feel the ache
and bruise and scrapes,
hands and fingers tired
and stripped raw as
I drag myself upward.
Always onward. You cannot
arrive if you never leave, a promise
balanced on the power in
the journey for a summit.
Grateful and tender, I can recall
my humanity. Quietly returned.
When I inevitably feel restlessness
building again like a storm
threatening my refuge of safety,
the primordial rock responds
from a distance, almost reproachful:
*do you not remember my gift?*

## RELEASED

The distinct sound of letting go is
that of rustling tree limbs in a summer breeze
while dressed in dusky peach sun-beams.
Wildlife undergoes a shift change,
the magical melody of creatures who
have their preferences to be announced
by sun or moon and bathe us
in lessons of forgiveness. A gift.
They join together in the foretelling
of unused hours – the possibilities for starting over.

# REINCARNATION

I can birth divinity; allow me to show you.
First, I eat the petals of a wild poppy flower,
their blood-red limbs delicate upon my tongue.
Then, I examine the body left behind, its spell
of sleep resting finely next to a bed of death.
My fingers hover across their stems, stalking,
deities built within me. Humming, vibrating:
I touch upon the gladiolus next as the unrelenting
August heat goads my tired, reddened skin.
I will not yield in my pruning, the colorful
perennials towering to meet my eyes in my
overgrown garden. Summer is a season for
the stubborn, and I stand with my defiant warriors.
Pinks and reds and oranges arrange themselves
in this field of resurrection: prepared, powerful.
They understand how gods will be buried here,
have been buried here, yielding their bodies.
Methodically, I continue to eat the holy.
I birth myself each year – divinity coating my
fingers as the young sprouts reach for my touch.
There are no gods before me as I behold my green
nursery and the potential that comes with dying.

# A ROOM FOR MY HALO

*poem with the final line from The Bell Jar*

I was swept away early in a forced rush
to an abandoned home of hauntings,
reproducing scenes and people I once knew –
still standing, still proud – unencumbered
though they brought me forth for dissection.
My life the meal that hung from their jowls,
a thorough display of apathetic gluttony.
There was an ask to devour all light as though I
were the cosmic reaction to a dying star,
an ask to absolve the traitors of the living. I have
been tempted by ghosts who offer dreams
of permanence in a whisper that curls in my ear
and wonders at my humanity. A vision comes
to mind. In the dark, the emptiness I felt was a moniker
for every pretend god seeking my body – smothered
and then shattered, temptresses of sins
that were distractions from the ruination at the hands
of the powerful and thus excused. Until now.
Memory is a gift for the hollow and I have been nothing
less than an excavator seeking treasure. I offer
revival in the expansion of my lungs, the evolving force
of my life, and reject solicitations of those
unfurling, then fading, in triviality. I seek the halo
surrounding other spaces, more compelling doors,
and turn the knob cautiously to a place not yet
cursed and gutted. A small gift, this light,
my request for renaissance held with my desires.
I glimpse inside towards the spark of what will be
so much more. The eyes and faces all turn themselves
towards me, and guiding myself by them,
as by a magical thread, I step into the room.

## HOPE

I can hear hands unclasping
in the night, the broken sigh
of prayers carrying on like birds,
sharp calls saying, *"I'm here, I'm here."*

## ASH BY ASH

The original sin:
punished for hunger
and refused the right to anger,
a poison carried forth by every woman hence.
When I listened to my fury,
it told me that hell was already here
but the world will outlast man's violence.
So I will free fall aflame into my power:
devouring my interim state and birthing
the goddess who is unafraid of her
wrath. The ash left behind will serve
as a salve for generations until
only the earth's wind remains,
unbothered by something so human
as sin.

## RITUAL

I have found little gods
in the vessels of my lungs.
How they create then push me.
There are little deities behind my eyes
that seek always for something, something.
Perhaps I am not ruined, they find.
There is a sentence that lives within me.
We all have one, the little gods say.
Perhaps it is the moss beneath aging rocks
or the reaching limbs of a longleaf pine
or maybe it is something more
internal, central, you know the way.
It is endless, the sentence, made up
by fragments that quirk with discovery.
Have you ever wondered what yours would be?
Whisper it now, little gods.
Call yourself by name.

# Acknowledgements

The last time I published anything, it was under a different name – my married name. Since then, my life has changed genres, as my friends and I like to joke, as I underwent radical mental health treatment, a divorce, and a lot of healing from all the previous chapters of my life. I don't necessarily regret any of it except perhaps ignoring all the signs I was not doing well, because I am obviously on a path now that I was always meant to be on. I started writing these poems around three years ago that were an attempt at processing… everything. I didn't know then that I was embarking on writing another book, but as I kept working, I noticed a distinct theme in my work. And I realized that even if I wasn't prepared to share this work with the world, the writing of it was necessary for me. I've never worked harder on a book. It's true what they say about this process: it is a labor of love. Perhaps sometimes even hatred, if I'm being honest.

But in the end, I am so proud of these poems because they encompass my journey the past several years – all the grief and pain, yes, but also all of the stubborn hope and defiant joy. I returned to nature throughout these years as well while I worked on this book, which is evident in the poems throughout. Being outdoors has always given me a sense of peace and that is something my life utterly lacked for a long while. I returned to hiking, began rock climbing, rediscovered biking, and started kayaking. The earth constantly offers us a humbling gift and though my own life is small by comparison, I can't help but feel it is in that smallness I can find my place in it. Yet another gift, one I hope to make the most of.

Thank you to my partner, Brandon, for listening to me rant and rave during the process and for always being my strongest supporter. Thank you all so much for reading this collection of poems. Thank you to all who dare to disturb the universe and create art. This is the stuff our lives are meant to be made up of.

# ABOUT THE AUTHOR

Ashley Logan (she/her) resides on a 3400-acre bird sanctuary in the woodlands of South Carolina with her partner and two dogs. She earned a Bachelor of Arts degree in English from the University of South Carolina in 2010 and has been published in various magazines over the years. When not writing, she enjoys traveling, hiking and rock climbing, buying too many books (even reading some of them), as well as dabbling in photography.

www.ingramcontent.com/pod-product-compliance
Lightning Source LLC
Chambersburg PA
CBHW060254150626
46553CB00019BA/2288